THE SIDE HUSTLE BLUEPRINT

Unlocking Wealth Through MLM

Henry Starks

Copyright © 2024 Henry Starks

All rights reserved

The characters and events portrayed in this book are fictitious. Any similarity to real persons, living or dead, is coincidental and not intended by the author.

No part of this book may be reproduced, or stored in a retrieval system, or transmitted in any form or by any means, electronic, mechanical, photocopying, recording, or otherwise, without express written permission of the publisher.

ISBN-13: 9798343074277

Cover design by: Henry Starks
Library of Congress Control Number: 2018675309
Printed in the United States of America

CONTENTS

Title Page
Copyright
Introduction
The Side Hustle Blueprint: 1
Chapter 1: Introduction to Side Hustles   2
The Appeal of Flexible Income Opportunities   4
Overview of Multi-Level Marketing   6
Chapter 2: The Basics of Multi-Level Marketing   8
What is MLM?   9
Key Terminology in MLM   11
How MLM Differs from Traditional Business Models   13
Chapter 3: Health and Wellness MLM   16
The Growing Health and Wellness Industry   17
Popular Health and Wellness MLM Companies   19
Building Your Brand in Health and Wellness MLM   21
Chapter 4: Financial Services and Investment MLM   23
The Importance of Financial Literacy   24
Types of Financial Services in MLM   26
Strategies for Success in Financial MLM   29
Chapter 5: Travel and Lifestyle MLM   31
Top Travel and Lifestyle MLM Companies   33

Promoting Travel Experiences Through MLM	35
Chapter 6: Digital Marketing Tools MLM	37
Essential Digital Marketing Tools for MLM	39
Building an Online Presence for Your MLM Business	41
Chapter 7: Education and Personal Development MLM	43
Popular Educational MLM Products	46
Techniques for Selling Educational MLM Products	48
Chapter 8: Building Your MLM Business	50
Creating a Business Plan for Your MLM	52
Networking and Building Relationships	54
Chapter 9: Overcoming Challenges in MLM	56
Managing Rejection and Setbacks	58
Staying Motivated and Focused	60
Chapter 10: Success Stories and Case Studies	62
Lessons Learned from Successful Side Hustlers	64
Key Takeaways for Aspiring MLM Entrepreneurs	66
Chapter 11: Conclusion and Next Steps	68
Creating Your Action Plan	70
Resources for Continued Learning and Support	72
Disclaimer	75
Affiliate Game	77

INTRODUCTION

With the rising cost of living and the desire for financial independence, more and more people are turning to side hustles to supplement their income. *The Side Hustle Blueprint: Unlocking Wealth Through MLM* is your go-to guide for building a successful side hustle through the power of Multi-Level Marketing (MLM). Whether you're new to MLM or looking to take your current efforts to the next level, this blueprint provides actionable insights, tips, and strategies to help you succeed.

From health and wellness products to digital marketing tools, this book covers the most lucrative MLM niches, showing you how to pick the right opportunities, grow your network, and maximize your income potential—all while maintaining a flexible work-life balance.

THE SIDE HUSTLE BLUEPRINT:

Unlocking Wealth Through MLM

CHAPTER 1: INTRODUCTION TO SIDE HUSTLES

Understanding the Side Hustle Economy

The side hustle economy has emerged as a significant aspect of modern financial life, allowing individuals to supplement their income while maintaining their primary jobs or responsibilities. This phenomenon is driven by a variety of factors, including the rising cost of living, the desire for financial independence, and the pursuit of personal passions. In this landscape, multi-level marketing (MLM) has gained traction as a viable option for those seeking flexible income opportunities. By leveraging social networks and personal connections, MLM allows individuals to build their own businesses with relatively low startup costs, making it accessible for a wide range of entrepreneurs.

In the realm of health and wellness MLM, the demand for products and services that promote a healthier lifestyle has never been higher. As consumers become more health-conscious, they seek out innovative solutions to improve their well-being. This presents a lucrative opportunity for side hustlers who can effectively market health and wellness products. By sharing their personal experiences and results, individuals can build trust and credibility within their networks, encouraging others to join them in their wellness journeys while also generating income through commissions and bonuses.

Financial services and investment MLM models cater to those looking to navigate the complex world of personal finance. With increasing numbers of individuals seeking guidance on budgeting, saving, and investing, this niche is ripe for opportunity. Side hustlers can empower others to take control of their financial futures, all while earning commission on the products and services they promote. By providing valuable information and resources, they can create a supportive community that fosters financial literacy and independence.

Travel and lifestyle MLM offers unique avenues for individuals who are passionate about exploration and adventure. This niche capitalizes on the increasing desire for experiential travel and lifestyle enhancement. Side hustlers can introduce their networks to exclusive travel deals, lifestyle products, and experiences that resonate with their audience. By creating engaging content and sharing personal travel stories, individuals can inspire others to pursue their travel dreams while simultaneously building a sustainable income stream through commissions on bookings and sales.

The digital marketing tools MLM sector has seen significant growth with the rise of online entrepreneurship. As more individuals turn to the internet to establish their businesses, they require effective marketing tools to reach their target audiences. Side hustlers can benefit from promoting software and services that help others grow their online presence. By educating their networks on the importance of digital marketing and sharing their success stories, they can drive interest and sales, all while enhancing their own skill set in the process. This symbiotic relationship between the side hustler and their audience ultimately fosters a thriving community of like-minded individuals pursuing financial success and personal growth.

THE APPEAL OF FLEXIBLE INCOME OPPORTUNITIES

The appeal of flexible income opportunities has become increasingly pronounced in today's dynamic economic landscape. As traditional employment models evolve, many individuals are seeking alternative revenue streams that offer both financial benefits and the flexibility to adapt to personal circumstances. Multi-level marketing (MLM) stands out prominently in this context, providing opportunities to generate income while balancing other commitments. This model enables participants to work at their own pace, making it especially attractive for side hustlers looking to supplement their income without the constraints of a conventional job.

Health and wellness MLMs exemplify the practical advantages of flexible income opportunities. With a growing consumer focus on health, wellness, and self-care, these ventures allow individuals to tap into a booming market. Participants can choose to work flexible hours, often promoting products they are passionate about and using social media platforms for marketing. This approach not only enhances their income potential but also fosters a sense of community among like-minded individuals who share similar health goals and interests.

In the financial services and investment niche, MLM offers unique opportunities for those with a knack for numbers and investment strategies. Individuals can engage with clients to provide financial advice, investment products, or insurance services while working on their own schedule. This flexibility allows participants to balance their professional responsibilities with personal commitments, creating a sustainable income model. Moreover, as they advance in the MLM structure, they can build teams that further leverage their income potential, creating a powerful avenue for growth and financial independence.

Travel and lifestyle MLMs present another compelling option for individuals seeking flexible income opportunities. This niche appeals to those with a passion for travel and exploration, allowing them to earn money while sharing their experiences. Participants can organize trips, promote travel packages, and build networks that enhance their income potential. The flexibility of working remotely enables individuals to manage their time effectively, making it easier to combine work with travel and leisure, ultimately leading to a fulfilling lifestyle.

Digital marketing tools and education-focused MLMs also contribute significantly to the appeal of flexible income opportunities. As more businesses shift online, individuals can capitalize on this trend by promoting digital marketing solutions or educational resources. These ventures often require minimal startup costs and offer extensive training, allowing participants to develop skills that can enhance their overall earning potential. The flexibility inherent in these opportunities provides individuals the chance to learn and grow while generating income, making them an ideal choice for those looking to diversify their revenue streams.

OVERVIEW OF MULTI-LEVEL MARKETING

Multi-level marketing (MLM) is a business model that allows individuals to earn income through direct sales of products or services while also recruiting others to join the sales force. This structure creates a network of distributors who earn commissions not only on their own sales but also on the sales made by their recruits, often referred to as their "downline." The appeal of MLM lies in its potential for passive income generation, allowing individuals to leverage their efforts through team-building and personal sales. It presents an opportunity for side hustlers to create a flexible income stream while working on their own terms.

In the context of health and wellness, MLM has gained significant traction, with many companies offering products such as dietary supplements, fitness programs, and skincare items. This niche is particularly attractive to consumers who are increasingly prioritizing their health and well-being. By participating in health and wellness MLM, side hustlers can tap into a growing market while promoting products that they are passionate about. The personal nature of these products often makes them easier to sell, as distributors can share their own experiences and outcomes with potential customers.

Financial services and investment MLMs offer another lucrative avenue for side hustlers. These companies typically provide services like insurance, investment advice, and financial planning tools. Given the growing interest in financial literacy and wealth building, individuals involved in this niche can position themselves as trusted advisors. By leveraging their knowledge and building a network of clients, they can create substantial income through commissions on services sold and ongoing customer relationships.

Travel and lifestyle MLM companies cater to the wanderlust of consumers, offering vacation packages, travel discounts, and lifestyle products. This niche appeals to side hustlers who enjoy traveling and want to share their experiences with others. By promoting travel-related products and services, distributors can earn commissions while helping others plan memorable experiences. The inspirational nature of travel can create a strong emotional connection, making it easier for distributors to engage with potential customers and build a loyal client base.

Digital marketing tools and education-focused MLMs provide opportunities for individuals interested in online entrepreneurship and personal development. These companies often offer training programs, software solutions, and resources designed to enhance business skills and personal growth. Participants can benefit from the educational content while also promoting valuable tools to others. This niche allows side hustlers to position themselves as experts while helping others improve their own skills and knowledge, creating a win-win situation that fosters both personal and professional growth.

CHAPTER 2: THE BASICS OF MULTI-LEVEL MARKETING

WHAT IS MLM?

Multi-level marketing (MLM) is a business model that has gained significant traction over the years as a viable strategy for individuals seeking flexible income opportunities. At its core, MLM allows individuals to earn income not only through their direct sales of products or services but also by recruiting others into the business. This creates a hierarchical structure where participants can earn commissions based on the sales made by their recruits, often referred to as their "downline." This dual income stream makes MLM an appealing option for side hustlers looking to supplement their primary income while enjoying the flexibility of working on their own terms.

In the realm of health and wellness, MLM has emerged as a popular niche, as consumers increasingly prioritize their well-being. Companies within this sector offer a range of products, from nutritional supplements to skincare solutions, allowing individuals to promote items they genuinely believe in. This personal connection to the products can enhance sales efforts and foster a sense of authenticity, which is critical in building lasting customer relationships. As a side hustler in health and wellness MLM, you can leverage your passion for fitness and health to connect with like-minded individuals, creating a community around your business.

Financial services and investment MLMs present another opportunity for individuals seeking to diversify their income streams. These companies typically offer services such as financial planning, investment advice, and insurance products. By becoming an independent representative, you can educate others about financial literacy while earning commissions on the services you sell. This niche not only allows you to build a business but also enables you to empower others to make informed financial decisions, thus creating a mutually beneficial relationship that can lead to sustained growth and income.

Travel and lifestyle MLMs cater to individuals passionate about exploration and experiences. These companies often provide travel packages, vacation clubs, or lifestyle products that enhance travel experiences. As a participant in this niche, you can share your travel experiences and insights, inspiring others to explore new destinations. The allure of travel combined with the financial incentives of MLM creates an engaging platform for side hustlers, allowing you to turn your passion for travel into a lucrative opportunity while sharing valuable experiences with a broader audience.

Digital marketing tools and education MLMs focus on providing resources for personal and professional development. With the rise of online businesses and the need for effective marketing strategies, these niches are booming. Participants can promote various tools, courses, and training programs that help individuals and businesses grow. By providing valuable content and education, you can establish yourself as an authority in your niche, attracting customers who are eager to learn and invest in their growth. This model not only offers financial rewards but also fulfills a deeper purpose of contributing to the development of others, making it a fulfilling side hustle for those passionate about education and empowerment.

KEY TERMINOLOGY IN MLM

Understanding the key terminology in multi-level marketing (MLM) is essential for anyone looking to navigate this business model effectively. MLM operates on a unique structure that distinguishes it from traditional sales methods. Familiarity with terms like "downline," "upline," "compensation plan," and "retail markup" can significantly impact the success of your venture in this dynamic market. By grasping these concepts, side hustlers can better position themselves to maximize their earnings and build sustainable businesses.

"Downline" refers to the individuals you recruit into your MLM organization, and their recruits, forming a hierarchical structure. Your downline represents the potential for earning commissions based on their sales and recruitment efforts. Conversely, "upline" describes those who recruited you, often providing essential support and mentorship. Understanding the relationship between these two terms is crucial, as the growth of your downline directly influences your income potential. This interconnectedness is a fundamental aspect of MLM that can lead to exponential earnings when managed effectively.

Another critical term is "compensation plan," which outlines how commissions and bonuses are structured within the MLM company. Each company may have a unique compensation plan, detailing how participants earn money based on sales volume, rank, and recruitment. For instance, some plans offer residual income, allowing participants to earn commissions on ongoing sales made by their downline. Familiarizing yourself with different compensation structures will empower you to choose the right MLM opportunity that aligns with your financial goals and personal values.

"Retail markup" is another essential concept in MLM, especially in niches like health and wellness or financial services. This term refers to the difference between the wholesale price at which a product is purchased and the retail price at which it is sold. Understanding retail markup is critical for setting competitive prices and maximizing profit margins. In sectors like travel and lifestyle MLM, where experiences are marketed, knowing how to price your offerings effectively can enhance customer satisfaction and boost your sales figures.

Finally, terms like "lead generation" and "duplication" play a significant role in successful MLM strategies. Lead generation refers to the process of attracting potential customers or recruits, often through digital marketing tools or social media platforms. Meanwhile, duplication is the ability to replicate successful practices within your downline, ensuring that your team can efficiently grow and thrive. By mastering these key terminologies, individuals in various niches can develop a robust understanding of MLM, allowing them to create effective strategies for building their side hustles and achieving financial independence.

HOW MLM DIFFERS FROM TRADITIONAL BUSINESS MODELS

Multi-level marketing (MLM) presents a distinct business model that diverges significantly from traditional business structures. Unlike conventional businesses, which typically rely on a linear distribution of goods or services, MLM operates on a network-based approach. In traditional models, companies sell products directly to consumers through established retail channels. In contrast, MLM encourages individuals to sell products while also recruiting others into the business, creating a tiered system where participants earn commissions based on their sales and the sales made by their recruits. This structure allows for potentially unlimited income based on individual effort and the growth of one's downline.

Another key difference lies in the initial investment and risk involved. Traditional businesses often require substantial capital to establish a storefront, inventory, and operational expenses. Entrepreneurs face significant financial risks before they see any return on their investment. Conversely, MLM typically requires a lower initial investment, making it an attractive option for side hustlers seeking additional revenue streams. Many MLM companies offer affordable start-up kits, which include products and training materials, allowing individuals to begin their business with minimal risk. This accessibility enables people from various backgrounds to participate, making MLM a viable option for those looking for flexible income opportunities.

The marketing strategies employed by MLMs also differ from traditional business models. In conventional businesses, marketing efforts are usually centralized and heavily rely on advertising through various channels such as television, print, or digital media. MLM, however, leverages the personal networks of its participants as a primary means of promotion. This word-of-mouth marketing can be highly effective, as individuals often trust recommendations from friends and family over traditional advertising. As a result, participants in MLM can build their customer base by fostering personal relationships, which can lead to higher conversion rates compared to typical marketing strategies.

Moreover, the compensation structure in MLMs is notably different from traditional businesses. In a conventional model, employees earn a fixed salary or hourly wage, with potential bonuses based on performance metrics. In MLM, however, income is primarily commission-based, which can lead to significant earnings for those who excel in sales and recruitment. This performance-based compensation structure incentives participants to be proactive in their efforts, aligning their income potential directly with their work ethic and commitment. While this can create significant rewards for top performers, it also means that earnings can be inconsistent and heavily influenced by individual performance.

Lastly, the community aspect of MLMs sets them apart from traditional business models. Many MLM companies foster a strong sense of community among their participants, often providing support through training, mentorship, and networking opportunities. This social component can be particularly appealing for side hustlers who may feel isolated in their entrepreneurial journey. Traditional businesses typically do not emphasize community in the same way; employees often work independently or within their own departments. In contrast, the collaborative environment of MLM can provide motivation and encouragement, helping individuals stay focused on their goals while building lasting relationships with like-minded entrepreneurs.

CHAPTER 3: HEALTH AND WELLNESS MLM

THE GROWING HEALTH AND WELLNESS INDUSTRY

The health and wellness industry has experienced significant growth in recent years, driven by an increasing awareness of personal well-being and a shift towards healthier lifestyles. This trend has been amplified by the rise of social media, where influencers and everyday consumers alike share their journeys toward better health. As people become more conscious of their physical and mental well-being, they are turning to a variety of products and services that cater to these needs. This growth presents a unique opportunity for side hustlers, particularly in the realm of multi-level marketing (MLM), as they can leverage this booming market to create additional revenue streams.

Health and wellness MLM companies offer a diverse range of products, from nutritional supplements and weight loss programs to skincare and fitness equipment. These offerings appeal to a broad audience, including those seeking to improve their health, beauty enthusiasts, and fitness buffs. By participating in health and wellness MLM, side hustlers can promote products that they are passionate about while building a network of customers and recruits. This not only provides financial benefits but also fosters a sense of community and shared goals among participants who are all striving for better health.

Moreover, the financial services and investment sectors within MLM also align well with the health and wellness industry. Many individuals are looking for ways to invest in their health, whether through better nutrition or preventive health measures. By combining health and wellness products with financial literacy and investment opportunities, MLM participants can create a comprehensive offering that addresses both physical well-being and financial security. This dual approach can attract a wider audience, making the business model more appealing to potential recruits and customers.

As the digital landscape continues to evolve, digital marketing tools MLM present an exciting avenue for growth within the health and wellness sector. With the rise of e-commerce, social media marketing, and online communities, side hustlers can effectively reach their target audience. Utilizing digital marketing strategies allows them to promote health and wellness products more efficiently, engage with customers, and build a loyal following. This approach not only enhances their ability to generate income but also empowers them to create valuable content that educates and inspires others on their health journeys.

Education and personal development MLM also play a crucial role in the growing health and wellness industry. Many individuals are seeking knowledge on how to lead healthier lives, manage stress, and cultivate positive habits. By offering educational resources and workshops alongside health and wellness products, side hustlers can position themselves as trusted experts in this space. This not only adds value to their business but also fosters long-term relationships with customers who are eager to learn and improve their lives. By tapping into these synergistic opportunities, side hustlers can thrive in the flourishing health and wellness industry.

POPULAR HEALTH AND WELLNESS MLM COMPANIES

In the realm of multi-level marketing (MLM), health and wellness companies have established themselves as some of the most prominent and lucrative options for side hustlers. These companies often promote a range of products, from dietary supplements to skincare, appealing to a broad audience that prioritizes health and well-being. Notable players in this sector include companies like Herbalife, Amway, and Isagenix. Each of these brands has built a robust reputation and a loyal customer base, making them attractive choices for individuals looking to supplement their income while promoting products that align with healthy lifestyles.

Herbalife, for instance, specializes in nutritional supplements and weight management products. With a global presence and a well-defined marketing strategy, it empowers its distributors through training and support. This company offers a straightforward business model that allows individuals to earn commissions based on product sales and recruitment. The emphasis on health and wellness not only resonates with consumers but also provides distributors with the opportunity to promote products they genuinely believe in, creating a sense of purpose in their side hustle.

Amway, another leader in the health and wellness MLM space,

offers a diverse range of products, including vitamins, personal care items, and home care solutions. Their extensive training programs and established infrastructure make it easier for new distributors to enter the market. Amway's focus on personal development and business training equips individuals with the skills needed to succeed, fostering a community of motivated entrepreneurs. This company's long-standing history in the MLM industry adds credibility and stability, making it a favored choice for those seeking additional revenue streams.

Isagenix stands out for its emphasis on providing solutions for weight loss and overall health improvement. Their product line is designed to cater to various health goals, making it appealing to a wide audience. The company places a strong emphasis on community, with events and online support that encourage collaboration among distributors. This sense of belonging can be a significant motivator for individuals looking to build their own business while connecting with others who share similar health and wellness objectives.

In addition to these well-known companies, numerous emerging health and wellness MLMs are gaining traction. These companies often focus on niche markets, such as organic or clean-label products, which appeal to increasingly health-conscious consumers. As the trend toward holistic health and wellness continues to grow, side hustlers have the opportunity to capitalize on the expanding market by aligning themselves with innovative brands that resonate with their values. By choosing to partner with reputable health and wellness MLM companies, individuals can create flexible income opportunities that not only enhance their financial stability but also support their passion for promoting healthy living.

BUILDING YOUR BRAND IN HEALTH AND WELLNESS MLM

Building a brand in the health and wellness multi-level marketing (MLM) space requires a strategic approach that emphasizes authenticity, expertise, and community engagement. In an industry where trust is paramount, your personal brand must reflect your values and commitment to helping others achieve their health and wellness goals. Start by defining your unique value proposition—what sets you apart from others in the market? This could be your personal journey with health and wellness, specific certifications, or a passion for holistic living. Articulating this clearly will resonate with potential customers and downline members who share similar aspirations.

Establishing credibility is essential in the health and wellness MLM sector. Consider sharing your knowledge through various platforms, such as social media, blogs, or webinars. Create informative content that addresses common health concerns, offers tips for healthy living, or explains the benefits of the products you promote. By positioning yourself as an expert, you not only build trust with your audience but also attract individuals who are genuinely interested in your products and business opportunity. Regularly engaging with your audience through Q&A sessions or live demonstrations can further solidify your reputation as a knowledgeable leader in the health and wellness community.

Networking is a crucial element in building your brand. Connect with like-minded individuals, health professionals, and influencers within the health and wellness niche. Attend industry events, webinars, and local meetups to expand your reach. Collaborating with others can provide mutual benefits—exposing both parties to new audiences and creating opportunities for joint ventures or promotional campaigns. Additionally, fostering relationships with customers and team members can lead to referrals and organic growth, as satisfied clients are likely to recommend your products and business to others.

In the digital age, your online presence plays a significant role in brand building. Utilize social media platforms to showcase your journey, share testimonials, and post engaging content that highlights the benefits of your health and wellness products. Consider creating a dedicated website or blog where you can share in-depth articles, success stories, and product reviews. Optimize your content for search engines to increase visibility and attract a broader audience. Effective digital marketing strategies, including email newsletters and targeted ads, can also help you reach potential customers and recruits, driving traffic to your brand.

Lastly, focus on building a supportive community around your brand. Encourage interaction among your customers and team members by creating groups or forums where they can share experiences, ask questions, and support one another. This sense of belonging can enhance customer loyalty and motivate your downline to engage actively in the business. By fostering a positive and inclusive environment, you not only strengthen your brand but also empower others to thrive within the health and wellness MLM space. Your brand should be a beacon of inspiration, encouraging others to embrace healthier lifestyles while achieving their financial goals.

CHAPTER 4: FINANCIAL SERVICES AND INVESTMENT MLM

THE IMPORTANCE OF FINANCIAL LITERACY

Financial literacy is an essential skill for anyone looking to navigate the complexities of managing their personal finances, especially for individuals engaged in side hustles or seeking additional revenue streams. Understanding fundamental financial concepts enables entrepreneurs, particularly those in multi-level marketing (MLM) industries, to make informed decisions that can significantly impact their success. A strong grasp of financial principles can lead to better budgeting, investment strategies, and overall financial management, allowing side hustlers to maximize their potential earnings while minimizing risks.

In the context of MLM, financial literacy helps individuals assess the viability of their business ventures. Many side hustlers are drawn to industries such as health and wellness, financial services, travel, and digital marketing tools, where understanding the financial landscape is crucial. Knowledge of cash flow management, profit margins, and return on investment can empower these entrepreneurs to evaluate their options critically. By mastering financial concepts, they can identify which products or services within their MLM structure are worth pursuing and which may not yield the desired returns.

Furthermore, financial literacy plays a vital role in setting realistic financial goals. Side hustlers need to establish clear objectives regarding their income expectations, savings targets, and investment plans. Without a solid understanding of financial principles, it is easy to fall into common traps, such as overestimating potential earnings or underestimating expenses. By learning to create actionable budgets and forecasts, individuals can develop a roadmap that aligns with their financial aspirations, ultimately enhancing their motivation and commitment to their side hustles.

Moreover, financial literacy equips side hustlers with the tools necessary to make sound investment decisions. Whether investing in marketing tools for their digital campaigns or participating in training programs for personal development, understanding the principles of risk and reward is essential. This knowledge allows entrepreneurs to evaluate opportunities critically and choose investments that align with their long-term financial goals. By cultivating a mindset focused on informed decision-making, side hustlers can avoid common pitfalls and build a sustainable income stream.

Finally, fostering financial literacy creates a culture of accountability and empowerment among side hustlers. When individuals share their financial knowledge and experiences, they contribute to a supportive community where everyone can learn and grow. This collective wisdom can lead to innovative approaches and strategies within the MLM space, benefiting all participants. As side hustlers become more adept at managing their finances, they not only enhance their prospects for personal success but also inspire others to pursue their goals with confidence and clarity.

TYPES OF FINANCIAL SERVICES IN MLM

Multi-level marketing (MLM) offers a diverse range of financial services that cater to various interests and niches, providing individuals with flexible income opportunities. Understanding the types of financial services available in MLM can help side hustlers identify which model aligns best with their personal goals and aspirations. Each category within MLM not only serves a specific market but also presents unique advantages and potential for income growth, making it essential for aspiring entrepreneurs to explore their options thoroughly.

In the health and wellness MLM sector, financial services often include nutritional products, supplements, and wellness programs. These services typically emphasize personal health improvements and lifestyle changes, allowing participants to earn commissions through direct sales and recruitment. Many health and wellness MLMs provide training and support, enabling representatives to build effective sales strategies. With a growing global focus on health and fitness, this niche presents an appealing opportunity for individuals passionate about promoting well-being while enhancing their financial security.

The financial services and investment MLM niche equips participants with knowledge and tools related to money management, investment strategies, and financial literacy. Companies in this category often offer products like insurance, investment plans, and retirement savings options. Side hustlers can benefit from the dual advantage of earning commissions on sales while also gaining expertise in financial planning. This sector not only provides income potential but also empowers individuals to make informed financial decisions, creating a win-win situation for representatives and their clients.

Travel and lifestyle MLM programs focus on offering travel-related products and services, such as vacation packages, travel memberships, and lifestyle experiences. Participants in this niche can earn commissions through sales and by recruiting others to join the program. This type of MLM appeals to individuals who are passionate about travel and experiences, allowing them to turn their interests into a profitable venture. Additionally, the travel industry has a vast customer base, providing ample opportunities for representatives to connect with potential clients and expand their networks.

Digital marketing tools MLMs provide services that facilitate online business growth, including website development, social media management, and digital advertising solutions. These companies often target aspiring entrepreneurs who seek to enhance their online presence and market their products effectively. Participants can earn income through sales of digital tools and by helping others set up their online businesses. This niche is particularly relevant in today's digital age, where online marketing is essential for success, making it an attractive option for those looking to capitalize on their marketing skills while generating additional revenue streams.

Education and personal development MLMs offer products centered around self-improvement, skill-building, and professional development. These services include courses, coaching programs, and mentorship opportunities aimed at enhancing personal and professional skills. Participants can earn commissions through both product sales and recruitment, fostering a community focused on growth and learning. This niche appeals to individuals passionate about helping others while also investing in their own development, creating a sustainable income model that reinforces continuous personal growth and success in various aspects of life.

STRATEGIES FOR SUCCESS IN FINANCIAL MLM

To achieve success in financial MLM, it is essential to understand the foundational strategies that can lead to sustainable growth and profitability. First and foremost, selecting the right MLM company is crucial. Prospective side hustlers should conduct thorough research on various companies within their chosen niche, assessing their compensation plans, product quality, and market demand. This initial step lays the groundwork for a successful venture, as partnering with a reputable company will provide the necessary support and resources to thrive in the competitive landscape of multi-level marketing.

Building a solid personal brand is another vital strategy for success in financial MLM. Individuals should leverage their unique strengths and experiences to create an authentic online presence. This involves utilizing social media platforms, personal websites, and blogs to share valuable content related to their niche, whether it be health and wellness, financial services, or digital marketing tools. By establishing themselves as knowledgeable and trustworthy figures within their field, side hustlers can attract potential customers and recruits, thereby expanding their reach and influence in the MLM space.

Networking plays a pivotal role in MLM success. Side hustlers should actively engage with their existing network while also seeking to expand it through community events, online forums, and industry webinars. Cultivating relationships with individuals who share similar interests or goals can lead to collaborative opportunities and referrals. Additionally, joining relevant groups on social media can help in gaining insights from experienced marketers and learning effective selling techniques, which are essential for building a successful MLM business.

Effective communication skills are paramount in financial MLM. Side hustlers must be able to articulate the value of their products and the opportunity their MLM business presents. This includes refining sales pitches, mastering objection handling, and fostering genuine connections with prospects. Utilizing storytelling techniques can also enhance the appeal of presentations, making them more relatable and compelling. Furthermore, ongoing training and personal development in sales and marketing skills will empower individuals to navigate challenges with confidence and adaptability.

Finally, maintaining a consistent and disciplined approach is essential for long-term success in financial MLM. Side hustlers should set realistic goals and develop a structured plan to achieve them. Regularly evaluating progress and adjusting strategies as needed will help in staying on track. Additionally, celebrating small victories can keep motivation levels high, reinforcing the commitment to the MLM journey. By combining persistence with strategic planning, individuals can unlock their potential for wealth and success through multi-level marketing, creating a rewarding side hustle that aligns with their lifestyle and financial aspirations.

CHAPTER 5: TRAVEL AND LIFESTYLE MLM

The Travel Industry and Its Opportunities

The travel industry presents a wealth of opportunities for individuals seeking to diversify their income streams through multi-level marketing (MLM). With the global travel market projected to grow significantly in the coming years, the potential for side hustlers to tap into this sector is immense. The rise of online travel agencies, personalized travel experiences, and niche travel markets has created a fertile landscape for MLM ventures. By aligning with a travel and lifestyle MLM, individuals can leverage their passion for travel while earning a commission from bookings and referrals.

One of the most appealing aspects of the travel industry is the flexibility it offers. Side hustlers can work on their own terms, choosing when and how much to invest in their travel MLM business. This adaptability is particularly beneficial for those juggling multiple commitments or seeking to supplement their primary income. With the ability to operate online, individuals can reach potential clients across various demographics, making it easier to build a diverse customer base. As travel becomes more accessible, connecting with clients who are eager to explore new destinations can lead to substantial financial rewards.

Health and wellness are increasingly intertwined with travel, creating additional opportunities within this niche. Many travelers seek wellness retreats, fitness vacations, and holistic travel experiences. MLM companies focused on health and wellness often promote travel packages that cater to these interests. By combining the growing awareness of health-conscious living with travel opportunities, side hustlers can tap into a lucrative market. This intersection allows individuals to promote packages that not only provide travel experiences but also foster a healthier lifestyle for their clients.

Financial services and investment MLMs can also find synergy with the travel industry. As people seek to invest in experiences rather than material possessions, financial planners can offer travel-related investment advice. This could involve promoting travel rewards credit cards, travel insurance, or investment opportunities in travel-related businesses. By positioning themselves as knowledgeable resources, individuals in this niche can generate leads and referrals, creating a continuous income stream linked to their travel offerings. The ability to provide financial guidance while promoting travel can enhance credibility and attract clients.

Digital marketing tools play a crucial role in promoting travel MLM opportunities. With the travel industry heavily reliant on online marketing, those adept in digital strategies can excel in this space. Utilizing social media, email marketing, and content creation can help side hustlers effectively reach their audience. Moreover, education and personal development MLMs can support this endeavor by offering training in digital marketing techniques. This combination of skills not only enhances the side hustler's ability to promote travel packages but also broadens their overall business acumen, ultimately leading to greater success in multiple revenue streams.

TOP TRAVEL AND LIFESTYLE MLM COMPANIES

The travel and lifestyle multi-level marketing (MLM) sector has gained significant traction among side hustlers seeking flexible income opportunities. This niche not only allows individuals to promote products and services they are passionate about but also offers the unique advantage of tapping into the ever-growing travel industry. As travel becomes increasingly accessible and desirable, MLM companies in this sector provide avenues for earning while enjoying the perks of travel-related experiences and products.

One of the leading companies in this space is WorldVentures, well-known for its focus on vacation and lifestyle products. Members can sell travel memberships that offer discounts on trips and accommodations, which appeals to travel enthusiasts. This model is attractive to individuals looking to monetize their love for travel while also providing value to their customers. WorldVentures' emphasis on building a community of like-minded travelers further enhances its appeal, creating a supportive environment for those just starting their side hustle journey.

Another notable player is Travelodge. This company offers a unique approach, combining travel accommodations with a robust MLM structure. Travelodge allows members to earn commissions not only through direct sales of lodging services but also by recruiting others into the business. This dual-income potential attracts many individuals who desire a flexible work-life balance and the ability to generate passive income through their network. The brand's reputation for quality and affordability also aids in the recruitment of new members, as it appeals to a broad audience seeking travel solutions.

In addition to these, companies like Vacation Travel and DreamTrips have carved out significant niches within the travel MLM market. Both brands focus on providing exclusive travel experiences, ranging from luxurious getaways to family-friendly vacations. They offer members the chance to earn through direct sales and team-building incentives, making it easier for individuals to grow their income through referrals. Such companies also leverage modern marketing techniques, including social media platforms, allowing members to promote their offerings in a way that resonates with potential customers.

The travel and lifestyle MLM sector continues to evolve, with innovative companies emerging to meet the demands of modern consumers. As side hustlers explore additional revenue streams, these businesses present an appealing opportunity. With the right approach, individuals can build a network, offer valuable products and experiences, and create a sustainable income source that aligns with their lifestyle goals. This approach not only enhances personal financial growth but also fosters a community of travel enthusiasts dedicated to exploring the world together.

PROMOTING TRAVEL EXPERIENCES THROUGH MLM

Promoting travel experiences through multi-level marketing (MLM) offers a unique opportunity for individuals seeking flexible income streams. This niche appeals not only to travel enthusiasts but also to those looking to leverage their passion for exploration into a profitable side hustle. In the context of MLM, travel experiences can range from vacation packages to exclusive travel clubs, allowing participants to earn commissions while sharing their adventures with others. By aligning personal travel experiences with the MLM model, individuals can create a compelling narrative that resonates with potential customers and recruits.

One of the key advantages of promoting travel through MLM is the ability to tap into an existing market of travel enthusiasts. Many people are eager to learn about new destinations, travel tips, and exclusive deals. As an MLM representative, you can position yourself as a knowledgeable resource, sharing insights and experiences that encourage others to consider travel opportunities. By utilizing social media platforms, blogs, or video content, you can create engaging material that showcases travel experiences and highlights the benefits of joining your MLM travel program. This approach not only builds your credibility but also attracts a community of like-minded individuals who are interested in both travel and business.

In addition to promoting travel experiences, MLM programs often come with a range of health and wellness products that can enhance the travel experience. For example, wellness supplements or travel-friendly health products can be marketed alongside travel packages, appealing to health-conscious consumers. By combining travel with health and wellness offerings, you can create comprehensive packages that cater to a diverse audience. This cross-promotion not only increases your revenue potential but also enhances the overall value proposition of your MLM business.

Financial services and investment opportunities within the MLM travel niche also present significant benefits. Many MLM travel programs incorporate financial literacy components, empowering individuals to manage their travel budgets effectively. By educating your audience on how to save for travel or invest in travel experiences, you position yourself as a trusted advisor. This approach can lead to increased engagement and loyalty, as customers appreciate the added value of financial guidance. Moreover, promoting travel as an investment in personal well-being can further resonate with those seeking a balanced lifestyle.

Finally, integrating digital marketing tools into your MLM travel promotion strategy can enhance reach and engagement. Utilizing online platforms allows for targeted advertising and the ability to track customer interactions. By harnessing the power of digital marketing, you can create tailored campaigns that speak directly to potential customers' interests and preferences. This targeted approach not only increases the likelihood of conversions but also fosters a sense of community among those who share a passion for travel. In conclusion, promoting travel experiences through MLM not only provides an avenue for income generation but also enriches lives through shared experiences and personal growth.

CHAPTER 6: DIGITAL MARKETING TOOLS MLM

The Role of Technology in MLM

The integration of technology into multi-level marketing (MLM) has transformed the landscape of this industry, making it more accessible and efficient for side hustlers seeking additional revenue streams. In the past, MLM largely relied on face-to-face interactions, home parties, and traditional marketing methods. However, the advent of digital platforms has enabled individuals to reach broader audiences without geographical limitations. Social media, for instance, has become a powerful tool for promoting products and attracting potential recruits, allowing MLM participants to connect with like-minded individuals and expand their networks quickly.

In the health and wellness sector of MLM, technology plays a crucial role in educating consumers about products. Online webinars, video tutorials, and interactive content have become essential in demonstrating the benefits of various health products. These digital resources not only help in building trust with potential customers but also empower MLM representatives with the knowledge they need to effectively communicate product advantages. Furthermore, customer relationship management (CRM) tools have streamlined communication and follow-ups, enabling representatives to manage their contacts more efficiently and enhance their sales strategies.

Financial services and investment MLMs have also benefited significantly from technological advancements. Online platforms allow for the easy dissemination of information regarding investment opportunities and financial education. Virtual meetings and digital presentations can simplify complex financial concepts, making them more digestible for potential clients. With the use of analytics and data-driven marketing techniques, MLM representatives can tailor their approaches based on market trends and customer preferences, leading to better engagement and conversion rates.

Travel and lifestyle MLMs leverage technology to provide immersive experiences and personalized service. Virtual tours, live-streamed events, and social media campaigns allow potential customers to envision themselves enjoying the travel experiences offered. Influencer marketing has gained traction in this niche, with representatives collaborating with social media influencers to reach broader audiences. Additionally, mobile apps and online booking systems streamline the process for customers, enhancing user experience and facilitating seamless transactions.

Digital marketing tools have become indispensable for all MLM niches, including education and personal development. Online courses and e-learning platforms offer representatives the ability to share valuable content while establishing themselves as industry experts. SEO strategies and content marketing can significantly increase visibility and attract potential customers. Automation tools for email marketing and social media posting help MLM representatives maintain consistent communication with their audience, ensuring that they remain engaged and informed. In summary, technology not only enhances the efficiency of MLM operations but also empowers side hustlers to build successful businesses in a flexible and innovative manner.

ESSENTIAL DIGITAL MARKETING TOOLS FOR MLM

In the rapidly evolving landscape of multi-level marketing (MLM), leveraging digital marketing tools is crucial for success. These tools not only streamline operations but also enhance your ability to reach and engage potential customers and recruits. For side hustlers in niches such as health and wellness, financial services, travel and lifestyle, and education, the right digital marketing tools can make a significant difference in building a sustainable and profitable MLM business.

One essential tool for any MLM entrepreneur is a customer relationship management (CRM) system. A CRM allows you to manage interactions with potential leads and existing customers efficiently. It helps track communication, follow-up schedules, and sales history, ensuring that no opportunity slips through the cracks. In health and wellness MLMs, for instance, a CRM can help you keep detailed records of client preferences and health goals, enabling personalized communication that fosters loyalty and retention.

Another vital category of tools is social media management platforms. These tools enable you to schedule posts, track engagement metrics, and analyze the performance of your content across various social networks. For those in travel and lifestyle MLMs, effective social media marketing can showcase experiences and generate leads. By using platforms like Hootsuite or Buffer, you can maintain a consistent online presence, engage with your audience, and promote your offerings without overwhelming your daily schedule.

Email marketing software is also crucial for nurturing relationships and driving conversions. Platforms such as Mailchimp or Constant Contact allow you to create targeted email campaigns tailored to the interests of your audience. For individuals in financial services and investment MLMs, sending out informative newsletters or valuable content can establish authority in your field while guiding prospects through the buying process. Segmenting your email lists based on specific demographics or behaviors can lead to higher engagement rates and conversions.

Lastly, analytics tools are essential for understanding your marketing effectiveness. Google Analytics and similar platforms provide insights into website traffic, user behavior, and campaign performance. This data is invaluable for adjusting strategies and optimizing campaigns in real-time. For side hustlers in education and personal development MLMs, utilizing analytics can help pinpoint which content resonates most with your audience, allowing for more focused and impactful marketing efforts.

By integrating these essential digital marketing tools into your MLM strategy, you can enhance your outreach, streamline processes, and ultimately drive growth. Embracing technology will not only save you time but also provide valuable insights into your marketing efforts, setting you on the path to financial success in your side hustle.

BUILDING AN ONLINE PRESENCE FOR YOUR MLM BUSINESS

Building an online presence is crucial for the success of any multi-level marketing (MLM) business. In today's digital age, potential customers and recruits increasingly turn to the internet to find information and connect with brands. Establishing a strong online presence not only enhances your visibility but also builds credibility and fosters relationships with your audience. For side hustlers in the MLM space, leveraging online platforms effectively can help attract new customers and recruits, ultimately driving sales and growth.

The first step in building an online presence is to create a professional website. Your website serves as a central hub for your MLM business, showcasing your products, services, and personal brand. It should include essential elements such as an engaging homepage, detailed product descriptions, and clear calls-to-action. Additionally, consider incorporating a blog where you can share valuable content related to your niche, such as health tips for wellness MLMs or investment strategies for financial services MLMs. This not only positions you as an authority in your field but also improves your search engine optimization (SEO), helping potential customers find you more easily.

Social media platforms are another vital component of your online presence. Channels like Facebook, Instagram, and LinkedIn allow you to connect with a broader audience and engage with them on a personal level. Choose the platforms that align with your target audience and create content that resonates with them. For instance, if you are in a travel and lifestyle MLM, share captivating travel stories and tips, while those in digital marketing tools MLMs can post tutorials and success stories. Regular interaction, whether through live videos, Q&A sessions, or responding to comments, helps build a community around your brand and keeps your audience engaged.

Email marketing is an effective strategy for maintaining communication with your audience and nurturing leads. Collect email addresses through your website and social media channels, and create a newsletter that provides valuable insights, exclusive offers, and product updates. Personalizing your emails can significantly improve engagement rates. By segmenting your audience based on their interests and behaviors, you can tailor your messages to meet their specific needs, whether they are potential recruits or customers interested in personal development resources.

Finally, consider utilizing online advertising to amplify your reach. Platforms like Facebook Ads and Google Ads allow you to target specific demographics, ensuring your marketing efforts reach the right audience. Experiment with different types of ads, such as video ads or carousel ads, to see what resonates best with your audience. Track your results using analytics tools to refine your strategies over time. By investing in online advertising, you can accelerate your growth and establish a robust online presence that supports your MLM business objectives.

CHAPTER 7: EDUCATION AND PERSONAL DEVELOPMENT MLM

The Demand for Personal Development

The demand for personal development has surged in recent years, driven by a growing recognition of its importance in achieving success across various life domains, including financial independence and entrepreneurial pursuits. For side hustlers and individuals seeking additional revenue streams, personal development serves as a crucial foundation. It equips them with the skills, mindset, and resilience needed to navigate the challenges of multi-level marketing (MLM) and other entrepreneurial ventures. As the world becomes increasingly interconnected, the ability to adapt, learn continuously, and cultivate a growth mindset is more vital than ever.

In the context of MLM, personal development encompasses a wide range of skills and knowledge areas. This includes effective communication, leadership, time management, and sales techniques. Individuals involved in health and wellness MLM, for instance, must not only understand their products but also develop the ability to inspire and motivate others to embrace healthier lifestyles. Similarly, those in financial services and investment MLM need a solid grasp of financial concepts as well as the ability to build trust and rapport with clients. Ultimately, personal development enhances the capacity of side hustlers to engage with their audience, resulting in stronger customer relationships and increased sales.

The rise of digital marketing has further emphasized the necessity of personal development in the MLM space. With the proliferation of online platforms and tools, individuals in travel and lifestyle MLM, for example, must harness social media and digital marketing strategies to reach potential customers effectively. This requires ongoing education and adaptation to new technologies and trends. Personal development in this context not only focuses on technical skills but also on cultivating creativity and innovation to stand out in a crowded marketplace. By investing in their own growth, side hustlers can position themselves as valuable resources within their networks.

Moreover, the education and personal development MLM niche has gained traction as individuals seek to enhance their skills and knowledge. This sector highlights the importance of lifelong learning and self-improvement. For side hustlers, engaging with personal development resources—such as courses, workshops, and coaching—can yield significant returns. By acquiring new expertise, they can diversify their offerings, appeal to broader audiences, and ultimately increase their income potential. This commitment to personal development not only benefits individual side hustlers but also contributes to the overall growth and credibility of the MLM industry.

In conclusion, the demand for personal development is a driving force behind the success of side hustlers in various MLM niches. As aspiring entrepreneurs recognize the need for continuous learning and skill enhancement, they are better equipped to navigate the complexities of their ventures. By prioritizing personal growth, individuals can unlock new opportunities for wealth and fulfillment, creating a sustainable path toward financial independence. The integration of personal development into their business strategies will empower side hustlers to thrive in an ever-evolving landscape, where adaptability and knowledge are key.

POPULAR EDUCATIONAL MLM PRODUCTS

In the realm of multi-level marketing (MLM), educational products hold a significant appeal for side hustlers seeking to diversify their income streams. These products often center around personal development, skill enhancement, and knowledge acquisition, making them attractive to individuals eager to invest in their growth while earning commissions. Popular educational MLM products include courses, coaching programs, and digital resources that empower individuals with valuable skills and insights, ranging from financial literacy to digital marketing strategies.

One notable category within educational MLM products is personal development courses. These programs often cover topics such as leadership, time management, and effective communication. Companies like Mindset Mastery and Success Academy offer courses that equip participants with the tools they need to succeed both personally and professionally. Affiliates earn commissions by promoting these courses, which resonate with a broad audience seeking self-improvement. As more people recognize the importance of personal growth, the demand for these educational products continues to rise.

In the financial services and investment sector, MLM companies are increasingly offering educational resources designed to enhance financial literacy. These products range from online seminars to comprehensive investment training programs. For instance, Wealth Builders Network provides a suite of resources that teach individuals how to manage their finances, invest wisely, and build wealth over time. Affiliates who promote these educational materials can tap into the growing interest in personal finance, making it a lucrative niche for side hustlers.

Travel and lifestyle MLMs also capitalize on the educational aspect by providing training and resources related to travel planning, budgeting, and lifestyle enhancement. Companies like TravelPro offer courses that teach individuals how to become successful travel agents, covering everything from booking techniques to customer service skills. These products not only empower affiliates to build their travel-related businesses but also attract customers who are interested in learning how to navigate the travel industry effectively.

Finally, digital marketing tools MLMs have emerged as a powerful source of educational products. With the rise of online entrepreneurship, many individuals are eager to learn how to market their businesses effectively in the digital landscape. Companies like Marketing Mastery provide comprehensive training programs and tools that cover social media marketing, SEO, and email marketing strategies. Affiliates who promote these products can leverage their own experiences in digital marketing to attract potential customers and build a thriving side hustle. By focusing on these popular educational MLM products, side hustlers can not only enhance their own skills but also create additional revenue streams through effective promotion.

TECHNIQUES FOR SELLING EDUCATIONAL MLM PRODUCTS

Understanding effective techniques for selling educational MLM products is crucial for side hustlers aiming to maximize their revenue potential. One of the foundational techniques is leveraging the power of storytelling. By sharing personal experiences or testimonials related to the educational product, sellers can create a relatable narrative that resonates with potential customers. This approach not only highlights the benefits of the product but also builds a connection with the audience, making them more likely to engage and make a purchase.

Another essential technique involves utilizing social media platforms to reach a broader audience. Platforms such as Facebook, Instagram, and LinkedIn are invaluable for promoting educational MLM products. Sellers should focus on creating engaging content that showcases the value of the products, such as informative posts, live demonstrations, or success stories. Additionally, joining relevant groups and communities can help in targeting individuals who are already interested in personal development and educational resources, thus increasing the chances of conversion.

Building a strong personal brand is also vital in the MLM space. Sellers should position themselves as knowledgeable experts in their niche, whether it's health and wellness, financial services, or digital marketing tools. This can be achieved by consistently sharing valuable insights, participating in webinars, and offering free resources related to the educational products they promote. When potential customers see a seller as a trusted authority, they are more likely to consider purchasing the products being offered.

Networking plays a significant role in selling educational MLM products. Attending industry events, webinars, and local meetups can help side hustlers connect with like-minded individuals and potential customers. During these interactions, sellers can discuss their products, share their successes, and build relationships that may lead to future sales. Additionally, forming partnerships with other MLM distributors can create opportunities for cross-promotion, further expanding the reach of their educational offerings.

Finally, incorporating follow-up strategies is crucial for nurturing leads and converting them into customers. After an initial interaction or presentation, sellers should maintain communication with potential clients through emails, phone calls, or social media messages. Providing additional resources, answering questions, and offering personalized recommendations can help keep the conversation going and demonstrate a commitment to helping the customer succeed. This ongoing engagement can ultimately lead to higher sales and a more robust customer base in the long run.

CHAPTER 8: BUILDING YOUR MLM BUSINESS

Identifying Your Target Market

Identifying your target market is a crucial step in building a successful multi-level marketing (MLM) business. Understanding who your ideal customers are will help you tailor your messaging, products, and marketing strategies effectively. The first step in identifying your target market is to analyze the demographics that align with your niche. For example, if you are in the health and wellness MLM space, your target market may include health-conscious individuals, fitness enthusiasts, or those seeking weight loss solutions. By understanding the age, gender, income level, and lifestyle preferences of your audience, you can create specific marketing campaigns that resonate with them.

Next, consider the psycho-graphics of your potential customers. This involves understanding their interests, values, and pain points. In the financial services and investment MLM niche, for instance, your target market may consist of individuals looking for additional income sources to secure their financial future. Identifying their motivations, whether it be financial security, retirement planning, or wealth accumulation, will allow you to position your offerings in a way that speaks directly to their needs. Researching forums, social media groups, and online communities related to your niche can provide insights into what potential customers are discussing and what challenges they face.

Moreover, segmenting your target market can help you refine your approach even further. Within the travel and lifestyle MLM niche, you might find distinct segments such as frequent travelers, adventure seekers, or individuals interested in luxury vacations. Each segment may have unique preferences and requirements, which means your marketing strategies should differ accordingly. By creating tailored marketing messages for each segment, you can enhance engagement and increase the likelihood of conversion.

In addition to demographics and psycho-graphics, it's essential to assess the competition within your niche. Understanding who your competitors are targeting will provide you with valuable insights into market gaps and opportunities. For the digital marketing tools MLM sector, you may discover that many competitors focus on small businesses. This knowledge could lead you to target freelancers or entrepreneurs who are just starting and may be overlooked by others. Analyzing competitor strategies can also inspire you to differentiate your brand and establish a unique selling proposition that appeals to your target market.

Finally, continually reassessing and refining your target market is key to long-term success. Market trends, consumer preferences, and technological advancements can shift over time, necessitating an adaptable approach. For those in the education and personal development MLM space, staying attuned to emerging trends or changes in learning methodologies will help you stay relevant. Regularly gathering feedback from your customers and analyzing your sales data can provide insights into how well you are meeting the needs of your target market. By being proactive in your market identification efforts, you can position your side hustle for sustained growth and success.

CREATING A BUSINESS PLAN FOR YOUR MLM

Creating a business plan for your MLM is a crucial step that sets the foundation for your success. A well-structured business plan not only clarifies your goals but also outlines the strategies you will implement to achieve them. Begin by defining your vision and mission statements, which should reflect the core values and objectives of your MLM venture. This initial step serves to remind you of your purpose and keeps you focused on your long-term aspirations, whether you are involved in health and wellness, financial services, travel, or digital marketing.

Next, conduct thorough market research to understand your target audience and competitors. Identify the demographics of the individuals you aim to reach, including their interests and pain points. This information will help you tailor your marketing strategies effectively. Analyze competitors within your niche to determine what works and what doesn't. By understanding their strengths and weaknesses, you can position your MLM business to fill gaps in the market and offer unique value propositions to your prospects.

Financial projections play a vital role in your business plan. Start by estimating initial investment costs, including supplies, marketing, and training expenses. Then, outline your revenue streams, taking into consideration product sales, commissions, and bonuses. Create a break-even analysis to determine how long it will take to cover your initial investment and start generating profit. This financial roadmap not only helps you stay on track but also serves as a useful tool if you seek funding or partnerships down the line.

Marketing strategies should be an integral part of your business plan. Consider various channels that are effective for your MLM niche, such as social media, email marketing, and webinars. Develop a content strategy that showcases your expertise and builds trust with potential customers. For instance, if you're involved in health and wellness, sharing testimonials, success stories, and educational content can engage your audience. Consistency and authenticity in your marketing efforts will strengthen your brand and attract more recruits and customers.

Lastly, outline your growth and scaling strategies. As your business begins to grow, consider how you will expand your reach and increase your revenue. This might involve diversifying your product offerings, exploring new markets, or investing in training and development for your team. Set measurable milestones to track your progress and regularly revisit your business plan to adapt to changing market conditions or personal goals. A dynamic business plan that evolves with your journey will keep you aligned with your vision and pave the way for sustained success in your MLM endeavor.

NETWORKING AND BUILDING RELATIONSHIPS

Networking and building relationships are essential skills for anyone pursuing success in multi-level marketing (MLM). In the context of MLM, your network is your net worth. Whether you are involved in health and wellness, financial services, travel, digital marketing tools, or personal development, establishing a strong network can significantly enhance your opportunities for growth and income. Building relationships within these niches not only helps you to gain insights and resources but also fosters a community that can provide support and motivation.

To start networking effectively, it is important to identify your target audience and the individuals who align with your goals. This involves researching potential partners, mentors, and clientele within your specific niche. Attend industry-related events, workshops, and seminars to connect with like-minded individuals. Utilize social media platforms such as LinkedIn, Facebook, and Instagram to engage with others in your field. Participate in discussions, share valuable content, and showcase your expertise. By actively engaging in these spaces, you can build a reputation as a knowledgeable and approachable resource in your niche.

Building genuine relationships is more than just exchanging business cards or social media follows. It requires consistent communication and a genuine interest in helping others succeed. Take the time to understand the needs and challenges of your contacts. Offer assistance, share resources, and celebrate their achievements. This reciprocity builds trust and loyalty, which are crucial in an MLM environment where personal referrals can lead to significant income. Remember that relationships are a two-way street; investing in others will often lead to them investing in you.

As you expand your network, leverage the power of mentorship. Seek out experienced professionals in your niche who can provide guidance and insights based on their own experiences. A mentor can help you navigate challenges, refine your strategies, and introduce you to key contacts. Additionally, consider becoming a mentor yourself. Sharing your knowledge and experiences not only reinforces your credibility but also expands your network as your mentees grow and connect with others in the industry.

Finally, remember that networking is an ongoing process. Stay in touch with your contacts, even if you are not currently working together. Regular check-ins, sharing valuable information, and inviting them to events can keep the relationship alive. As your network grows, so does your potential for income and opportunities in MLM. By prioritizing networking and relationship-building, you create a robust foundation for your side hustle, helping you unlock the wealth and flexibility you seek.

CHAPTER 9: OVERCOMING CHALLENGES IN MLM

Common Misconceptions About MLM

Many individuals harbor misconceptions about multi-level marketing (MLM) that can deter them from exploring this viable avenue for additional income. One prevalent myth is that MLM is synonymous with pyramid schemes. While both structures involve recruiting others, MLM is a legitimate business model where products or services are sold directly to consumers, and commissions are earned based on sales rather than solely on recruitment. Understanding this distinction is crucial for side hustlers looking to differentiate between a legitimate MLM opportunity and an illegal scheme, ensuring a safer and more informed approach to their potential ventures.

Another common misconception is that success in MLM is solely a result of personal selling skills. While effective sales techniques can certainly enhance performance, the reality is that success in MLM often hinges on the strength of the network and the support system within the organization. Effective training, mentorship, and community engagement play significant roles in nurturing new recruits and helping them build their own networks. Side hustlers should focus on finding companies that provide comprehensive training and resources, as these elements can significantly increase the likelihood of success.

Many people believe that MLM requires a massive initial investment or that it is only suitable for those with extensive business experience. In fact, many reputable MLM companies offer low start-up costs, making it accessible to a wider range of individuals, including those who may be new to entrepreneurship. Furthermore, many MLM organizations provide training and support that cater to various skill levels, allowing individuals to gradually enhance their business acumen while they grow their enterprises. This accessibility makes MLM an attractive option for those seeking flexible income opportunities without the burden of significant financial risk.

Another misconception is that MLM participants cannot achieve substantial income unless they operate full-time. While it is true that dedicating more time can lead to greater rewards, many successful MLM participants operate their businesses part-time while balancing other commitments. The flexibility of MLM allows side hustlers to tailor their efforts based on their schedules and personal goals. This adaptability can be particularly appealing to individuals exploring additional revenue streams without sacrificing their primary responsibilities.

Lastly, the notion that MLM is a quick path to wealth is misleading. Like any business endeavor, success in MLM requires time, effort, and persistence. Many individuals enter the MLM space with unrealistic expectations, expecting immediate financial returns. In reality, building a sustainable income through MLM involves establishing relationships, developing a customer base, and nurturing a team over time. By approaching MLM with a long-term mindset and a commitment to consistent effort, side hustlers can maximize their potential for success and create a rewarding income stream that complements their lives.

MANAGING REJECTION AND SETBACKS

Managing rejection and setbacks is an essential skill for anyone involved in multi-level marketing (MLM), as these experiences are often part of the journey toward success. In MLM, rejection may come from potential recruits or customers who may not see the value in your product or opportunity. Rather than viewing these encounters as personal failures, it's important to re-frame them as opportunities for growth. Understanding that rejection is a common experience in sales can help you build resilience and maintain motivation.

One effective strategy for managing rejection is to develop a positive mindset. When faced with setbacks, remind yourself that every successful individual has faced challenges and disappointments. Instead of dwelling on negative outcomes, focus on what you can learn from each experience. This can involve analyzing your approach, seeking feedback, or simply acknowledging that not everyone will be interested in what you have to offer. Embracing a growth mindset allows you to view each rejection as a stepping stone toward improvement, rather than a roadblock.

Another important aspect of managing setbacks is building a robust support system. Surrounding yourself with like-minded individuals who understand the challenges of MLM can provide encouragement and motivation during tough times. Joining networking groups, attending seminars, or participating in online forums can create opportunities for sharing experiences and strategies. Hearing success stories from others can also help you maintain perspective and remind you that perseverance often pays off in the long run.

Setting realistic goals is crucial in overcoming the emotional toll of rejection. Establishing achievable milestones can provide a sense of accomplishment and help you measure progress, even in the face of setbacks. By breaking your larger objectives into smaller, manageable tasks, you can celebrate small wins along the way. This approach not only helps to maintain motivation but also cultivates a sense of purpose, making it easier to navigate the ups and downs of your MLM journey.

Finally, practicing self-care can significantly enhance your ability to cope with rejection and setbacks. Engaging in activities that promote mental and emotional well-being, such as exercise, meditation, or hobbies, can help reduce stress and prevent burnout. Taking time to recharge can provide you with a fresh perspective and renewed energy to tackle challenges head-on. By prioritizing self-care, you position yourself to handle the inevitable rejections and setbacks of MLM with resilience and determination, ultimately steering your side hustle toward success.

STAYING MOTIVATED AND FOCUSED

Staying motivated and focused is crucial for anyone engaged in a side hustle, particularly in the realm of multi-level marketing (MLM). The journey can be challenging, filled with ups and downs, and often requires a significant amount of self-discipline. Establishing a clear vision of your goals is the first step to maintaining motivation. Visualize the lifestyle you aspire to achieve through your MLM efforts, whether it's financial freedom, a more flexible schedule, or the ability to travel extensively. Keeping this vision at the forefront of your mind can serve as a powerful motivator, encouraging you to push through the obstacles you might encounter along the way.

Creating a structured routine can also contribute significantly to maintaining focus. Allocate specific times each day dedicated to your MLM activities, whether it involves prospecting new leads, conducting presentations, or developing your personal brand. By treating your side hustle like a legitimate business, you instill a sense of professionalism and commitment that can drive your success. Additionally, integrating productivity techniques, such as the Pomodoro Technique or time blocking, can help you maximize your efficiency during these dedicated work periods, ensuring that you are making the most of your time.

Accountability plays a vital role in staying motivated. Surrounding yourself with a supportive network can enhance your commitment to your goals. Engage with fellow MLM participants, either through local meetups or online communities, to share experiences, celebrate successes, and offer encouragement during tough times. Establishing accountability partnerships can also be beneficial; consider finding a mentor or a fellow side hustler who can check in on your progress and provide constructive feedback. This collaborative mindset fosters an environment where motivation thrives, and you are less likely to succumb to isolation or self-doubt.

Continuing education and personal development are essential for keeping your enthusiasm alive. Many successful MLM professionals emphasize the importance of ongoing learning, whether through books, webinars, or workshops related to your niche. The health and wellness sector, for example, is constantly evolving, and staying informed about the latest trends and products can enhance your credibility and effectiveness. Moreover, personal development resources can equip you with the mindset tools necessary to overcome challenges and maintain a positive outlook, reinforcing your dedication to your side hustle.

Finally, celebrating your achievements, no matter how small, can significantly boost your motivation levels. Recognizing milestones along your journey—such as landing your first customer, achieving a sales target, or completing a training module—provides a sense of accomplishment that can propel you forward. Consider keeping a journal to document these successes and reflect on your growth. This practice not only reinforces your progress but also serves as a reminder of your capabilities during challenging times. By consistently nurturing your motivation and focus, you can unlock the potential of your MLM side hustle and move closer to your financial and personal goals.

CHAPTER 10: SUCCESS STORIES AND CASE STUDIES

Inspiring MLM Success Stories

In the realm of multi-level marketing, countless individuals have transformed their lives through determination, strategic planning, and effective execution. These inspiring MLM success stories serve as a testament to the potential that this business model holds for those willing to invest time and effort. From stay-at-home parents to corporate professionals seeking additional income, many have embraced MLM as a viable side hustle. Their journeys illustrate how leveraging a well-structured MLM opportunity can lead to financial independence and personal growth.

One noteworthy story is that of a former school teacher who turned to a health and wellness MLM after feeling unfulfilled in her traditional job. She was drawn to the company's mission of promoting healthy lifestyles and quickly recognized the potential for income while helping others. By utilizing her teaching skills, she effectively educated her network about the products and the business model. Within a year, she transitioned from part-time to full-time MLM engagement, replacing her teacher's salary and gaining the flexibility to spend more time with her family. Her success highlights how passion combined with strategic outreach can yield remarkable results in the health and wellness sector.

In the financial services and investment MLM niche, an individual with a background in finance began his journey with a major firm. Unsatisfied with the corporate structure, he sought an alternative that would allow him to work independently while helping others achieve financial literacy. By leveraging his expertise, he built a robust network of clients who valued his knowledge. Through workshops and personalized consultations, he not only increased his income but also empowered others to take control of their financial futures. His story underscores the importance of utilizing one's skills to create a fulfilling and profitable MLM venture.

The travel and lifestyle MLM sector is another area where individuals have found remarkable success. A couple passionate about travel decided to join a travel MLM, enabling them to explore the world while building a business. They shared their adventures on social media, captivating an audience eager to learn about various destinations and travel opportunities. Their authentic storytelling attracted a vast network of followers, leading to substantial income through commissions and bonuses. This example illustrates how blending personal interests with business can create an engaging and lucrative side hustle.

In the ever-evolving world of digital marketing tools MLM, a young entrepreneur discovered the power of online marketing strategies. Initially struggling to make ends meet, she invested in a digital marketing MLM that offered comprehensive training and tools. By applying her newfound skills, she expanded her reach and effectively marketed products online. Within months, she built a successful team, generating significant passive income. Her journey emphasizes the importance of continuous learning and adaptation in the digital age, proving that anyone can achieve success in MLM with the right mindset and resources.

LESSONS LEARNED FROM SUCCESSFUL SIDE HUSTLERS

Successful side hustlers often share common traits and strategies that can provide valuable insights for those looking to enhance their income through multi-level marketing (MLM). One of the most critical lessons is the importance of establishing a solid foundation of knowledge about the products and services being offered. Whether in health and wellness, financial services, or digital marketing tools, understanding the intricacies of the offerings not only builds credibility but also helps in effectively communicating their value to potential customers and recruits. This deep knowledge allows side hustlers to answer questions confidently and tailor their pitches to the needs of their audience.

Networking plays a vital role in the success of side hustlers. Many successful individuals in the MLM industry emphasize the power of building relationships both online and offline. Engaging with potential clients and fellow distributors creates a supportive community that can lead to increased sales and recruitment opportunities. By attending industry events, participating in webinars, and utilizing social media platforms, side hustlers can expand their reach and establish connections that may lead to future collaborations or mentorships. These relationships are not only beneficial for business growth but also provide moral support and motivation during challenging times.

Time management is another lesson that successful side hustlers often highlight. Balancing a side hustle with other commitments requires effective prioritization and organization. Successful individuals typically set aside specific time blocks dedicated to their MLM activities, including prospecting, training, and follow-ups. Utilizing tools such as calendars and productivity apps can help in staying on track and ensuring that the side hustle does not interfere with personal or professional responsibilities. This disciplined approach allows side hustlers to maximize their productivity and maintain a healthy work-life balance.

Adaptability is a crucial characteristic that successful side hustlers possess. The MLM landscape is continually evolving, and those who can pivot in response to market trends or changes in consumer behavior are more likely to thrive. This can involve staying updated on industry news, embracing new digital marketing strategies, or even altering product offerings to meet shifting demands. Successful side hustlers often engage in continuous learning, attending workshops and reading relevant literature to enhance their skills and knowledge. This commitment to growth not only benefits their own businesses but also positions them as informed leaders within their networks.

Lastly, resilience stands out as a key lesson from successful side hustlers. The journey to building a profitable side hustle is often fraught with challenges, including rejection and slow initial growth. Those who succeed tend to view setbacks as opportunities for learning rather than as failures. This mindset fosters perseverance and encourages individuals to refine their approaches rather than abandon their goals. Successful side hustlers often share stories of their struggles, emphasizing the importance of maintaining a positive outlook and remaining committed to their vision. By cultivating resilience, side hustlers can navigate obstacles and ultimately achieve sustained success in their MLM ventures.

KEY TAKEAWAYS FOR ASPIRING MLM ENTREPRENEURS

Aspiring MLM entrepreneurs should focus on several key takeaways that can significantly enhance their chances of success in this dynamic industry. First and foremost, understanding the product or service you represent is crucial. Whether you are involved in health and wellness, financial services, travel, or personal development, having a deep knowledge of your offerings allows you to convey their benefits effectively to potential customers and recruits. This knowledge not only builds credibility but also helps you to address any questions or concerns that prospects may have, making them more likely to engage with you.

Another essential takeaway is the importance of building a strong network. MLM relies heavily on relationships and personal connections. Start by tapping into your existing network of friends, family, and acquaintances. However, don't limit yourself to just your immediate circle. Attend networking events, join online communities related to your niche, and leverage social media platforms to expand your reach. The more robust your network, the greater your potential for generating leads and sales. Remember, every interaction is an opportunity to share your business and potentially recruit new team members.

Additionally, setting clear goals and tracking your progress is vital for maintaining motivation and direction. Define what success looks like for you, whether that means achieving a specific income level, recruiting a certain number of team members, or reaching a particular sales target. Use tools and resources available in the MLM industry to monitor your performance. Regularly reviewing your goals and progress will not only keep you accountable but also allow you to adjust your strategies as needed, ensuring you stay on the path to achieving your objectives.

Moreover, embracing continuous learning is a cornerstone of thriving in MLM. The industry is ever-evolving, and staying updated on the latest trends, marketing strategies, and best practices is essential. Invest in personal development through books, webinars, and training programs specifically focused on MLM. Many successful entrepreneurs attribute their achievements to the knowledge they gained from ongoing education. By continually improving your skills and understanding of the market, you can adapt to changes and maintain a competitive edge.

Lastly, cultivating resilience and a positive mindset is essential for anyone venturing into MLM. The journey will undoubtedly include challenges and setbacks, but maintaining a solution-oriented attitude can make all the difference. Surround yourself with supportive individuals who inspire you, and don't hesitate to seek mentorship from those who have succeeded in the field. Remember that persistence is key; many successful MLM entrepreneurs faced numerous obstacles before achieving their goals. By staying committed and resilient, you can navigate the ups and downs of the MLM world and ultimately unlock the wealth and flexibility you desire.

CHAPTER 11: CONCLUSION AND NEXT STEPS

Recap of Key Concepts

Recapping the key concepts is essential for reinforcing the foundations laid throughout "The Side Hustle Blueprint: Unlocking Wealth Through MLM." Understanding multi-level marketing (MLM) as a viable avenue for generating additional income is pivotal. MLM operates on a unique structure where individuals earn commissions not only through their sales but also through the sales made by their recruits. This framework creates a continuous income potential, enabling side hustlers to scale their earnings over time. Recognizing how this system functions can empower individuals to leverage their networks effectively and build a sustainable revenue stream.

Health and wellness MLM is a prominent niche that has gained traction among entrepreneurs seeking flexible income opportunities. The appeal of health and wellness products—ranging from supplements to fitness programs—aligns with a growing consumer interest in personal well-being. A successful venture in this sector requires an understanding of the target market, effective marketing strategies, and the ability to build a community around health-conscious living. By promoting products that resonate with their values, side hustlers can not only enhance their credibility but also drive sales through authentic engagement.

Financial services and investment MLM presents a different landscape but offers substantial opportunities for those knowledgeable in finance. This niche allows individuals to promote financial literacy, investment strategies, and wealth-building tools. Side hustlers venturing into this space must be well-versed in regulatory compliance and possess a strong grasp of financial products to build trust with potential clients. By providing valuable insights and offering tailored solutions, individuals can carve out a niche that not only generates income but also educates others about sound financial practices.

Travel and lifestyle MLM appeals to those with a passion for exploration and experiential living. This sector allows side hustlers to promote travel packages, lifestyle products, and experiences that enrich the lives of others. The key to success in this niche lies in storytelling and the ability to convey the transformative nature of travel. By sharing personal experiences and cultivating a sense of community around shared interests, individuals can effectively market these products while simultaneously enjoying the benefits of the lifestyle they promote.

Digital marketing tools MLM is crucial in today's technology-driven world, where online presence and visibility are paramount for success. This niche encompasses a range of products designed to help individuals and businesses optimize their marketing efforts. Side hustlers looking to excel in this area must stay updated on the latest digital marketing trends and tools. By providing value through education and support, they can foster a loyal customer base and drive sales. Education and personal development MLM further complements this by focusing on self-improvement resources, creating an ecosystem where individuals support each other in achieving their goals while generating income. Together, these concepts form a robust framework for building a successful side hustle in the MLM space.

CREATING YOUR ACTION PLAN

Creating your action plan is a crucial step for anyone venturing into multi-level marketing (MLM) as a side hustle. This structured approach will enable you to outline your goals, resources, and strategies to ensure that your efforts translate into tangible results. Start by defining your objectives. What do you hope to achieve through your MLM business? Whether your aim is to generate supplemental income, replace your current job, or build a long-term enterprise, having clear goals will guide your actions and decisions.

Next, assess your strengths and weaknesses as they relate to the specific niche you are pursuing. If you are interested in health and wellness MLM, consider your knowledge of the industry and how it can benefit your potential customers. Similarly, if your focus is on financial services, evaluate your expertise in investments and whether you can effectively communicate this to your audience. Understanding your unique selling proposition will help you stand out in a crowded market and attract the right customers to your business.

Once you have a grasp of your objectives and personal strengths, outline the specific steps you need to take to reach your goals. This includes identifying potential products or services to promote, selecting the right MLM company that aligns with your values, and creating a marketing strategy that resonates with your target audience. For instance, if you are pursuing travel and lifestyle MLM, consider how you can showcase experiences rather than just products. Developing a comprehensive plan will keep you organized and focused as you progress.

Another essential aspect of your action plan is to establish a timeline for achieving your objectives. Break down your goals into smaller, achievable milestones that can be tracked over time. This may involve setting weekly or monthly targets for sales, recruitment, or personal development. By creating a timeline, you can maintain motivation and adjust your strategies as needed, ensuring that you stay on course to achieve your overarching goals.

Finally, it is important to build a support network that can help you stay accountable and motivated throughout your journey. Engage with other side hustlers in the MLM space, whether through online forums, social media groups, or local meetups. Sharing experiences and challenges can provide valuable insights and encouragement. Additionally, consider seeking mentorship from successful individuals in your niche, as their guidance can help you navigate obstacles and refine your action plan over time. With a well-structured action plan and a supportive community, you can unlock the wealth potential of your MLM endeavors.

RESOURCES FOR CONTINUED LEARNING AND SUPPORT

In the ever-evolving landscape of multi-level marketing (MLM), continued learning and support are crucial for sustained success and growth. Many resources are available to side hustlers seeking to enhance their knowledge and skills in various niches, including health and wellness, financial services, travel, digital marketing, and education. Taking advantage of these resources can equip individuals with the tools necessary to thrive in their chosen MLM field.

Online courses and webinars are excellent avenues for furthering education in MLM. Platforms such as Udemy, Coursera, and LinkedIn Learning offer courses specifically tailored to multi-level marketing strategies, digital marketing techniques, and niche-specific training. These courses often feature industry experts who share valuable insights and best practices. Additionally, many MLM companies provide their own training programs that focus on product knowledge, sales techniques, and team-building strategies, making it essential for side hustlers to engage in these offerings for maximum benefit.

Networking remains an invaluable aspect of continued learning. Joining MLM-focused groups on social media platforms like

Facebook, LinkedIn, and Instagram can provide access to a wealth of shared experiences and advice from fellow side hustlers. Participating in these communities allows individuals to ask questions, share successes, and troubleshoot challenges. Attending industry conferences and local meetups also fosters connections with like-minded individuals and seasoned professionals who can offer mentorship and support.

Books and podcasts dedicated to MLM and entrepreneurship further serve as valuable resources for personal development. Renowned authors and successful MLM leaders have published numerous books that cover various aspects of building a thriving side hustle. These texts often delve into mindset, marketing strategies, and personal growth. Similarly, podcasts present an opportunity for on-the-go learning, featuring interviews with top earners in the industry who share their journeys and insights, thus inspiring and educating listeners.

Finally, utilizing digital tools and platforms can significantly enhance one's MLM venture. CRM (Customer Relationship Management) systems, social media management tools, and email marketing platforms can streamline operations and improve communication with team members and customers. Many software solutions offer tutorials and customer support to help users maximize their effectiveness. By embracing these technological resources, side hustlers can stay organized, track progress, and ultimately achieve their revenue goals more efficiently.

HENRY STARKS

DISCLAIMER

This ebook is intended for informational and educational purposes only. The strategies, techniques, and advice outlined are based on the author's personal experiences and research within the multi-level marketing (MLM) industry. Results may vary depending on individual effort, market conditions, and other external factors. While the content aims to provide guidance for success in MLM, there are no guarantees of income, business growth, or financial results.

MLM opportunities may involve inherent risks, and participants are encouraged to conduct thorough research and due diligence before joining any MLM business or network. The author and publisher are not liable for any losses or damages arising from the use of this ebook's content. Readers are responsible for any decisions or actions taken based on the information provided.

This ebook does not endorse or promote any specific MLM company or product and does not serve as legal, financial, or professional business advice. Please consult with appropriate professionals if you require assistance in these areas.

AFFILIATE GAME

"Affiliate Game" is an essential book series for anyone looking to master the art of affiliate marketing. Each volume dives deep into different facets of affiliate marketing, from the basics of setting up a successful affiliate site to advanced strategies for driving traffic and maximizing earnings.

With a focus on practical, actionable content, the series covers everything from choosing the right products and partners to leveraging social media and SEO to boost your affiliate efforts. Readers will learn how to create compelling content, convert visitors into buyers, and build a sustainable income stream through affiliate marketing.

Perfect for beginners and experienced marketers alike, "Affiliate Game" offers a thorough exploration of the tools and tactics needed to thrive in the competitive world of affiliate marketing. Tap into the expertise shared in these books, and start playing the affiliate game like a pro, ready to profit and grow in this dynamic field.

Blogging For Bucks: Seo Techniques To Boost Affiliate Earnings

Affiliate marketing is one of the most powerful ways to monetize a blog, but succeeding in this space requires more than just putting up links. To truly profit, you need to combine SEO mastery with strategic content creation. With the right approach, even small blogs can become highly profitable affiliate platforms. "Blogging for Bucks" guides you step by step through choosing profitable niches, driving organic traffic, and optimizing your blog for maximum conversion.

Are you tired of blogging without seeing significant income? "Blogging for Bucks" unlocks the secrets to turning your blog into a powerful income stream through affiliate marketing and SEO. Whether you're just starting out or looking to refine your strategies, this ebook provides actionable insights that can take your earnings to the next level.

Learn how to identify profitable niches, optimize your content for search engines, and boost conversions with compelling affiliate promotions. The book covers everything from keyword research to creating content that converts, all while ensuring you align your efforts with affiliate products that resonate with your audience.

www.ingramcontent.com/pod-product-compliance
Lightning Source LLC
Chambersburg PA
CBHW070353230526
45471CB00006B/2550